Marmaduke's

Size

Karen Bryant-Mole

D0452927

Evans

Marmaduke's Maths

Counting • Pattern • Shape • Size
Sorting • Where is Marmaduke?

Published by Evans Brothers Limited
2A Portman Mansions
Chiltern Street
London W1M 1LE

© BryantMole Books 1999

First published in 1999
First published in paperback 1999

Printed in Hong Kong by Wing King Tong Co Ltd

British Library Cataloguing in Publication Data

Bryant-Mole, Karen
  Size. - (Marmaduke's Maths)
  1.Marmaduke (Fictitious character) - Juvenile literature
  2.Mensuration - Juvenile literature
  I.Title
  530.8'1

  ISBN 0 237 52124 5

The name **Marmaduke** is a registered trade mark.

Created by Karen Bryant-Mole
Photographed by Zul Mukhida
Designed by Jean Wheeler
Teddy bear by Merrythought Ltd

About this book

Marmaduke the bear helps children to understand mathematical concepts by guiding them through the learning process in a fun, friendly way.

This book introduces children to the concept of size. It helps children learn about opposite pairs of size words by describing two similar objects. The words are then introduced in their comparative form, encouraging children to think of the objects in relation to the size of the one constant throughout the book, Marmaduke.

You can use this book as a starting point for further work on size. When comparing two objects, it helps if both objects are aligned. This will enable children to make accurate comparisons. If you want to see which of two necklaces is the longer, align them so that one end of one is directly above one end of the other. This helps children to see and understand that the longer necklace is the one that extends beyond the other.

contents

size

Marmaduke is playing with his toys.

My toys are different sizes.

Toys can be small or big, short or tall, narrow or wide.

Words like these are used to describe size.

Marmaduke is going to help you understand what they mean.

tall and short

Tall and short are to do with how high things are.

The green bottle is tall. The blue bottle is short.

a short hat

a tall hat

a tall candle

a short candle

7

taller and shorter

This plant is taller than me.

long and short

Long and short are to do with the size of things from one end to the other.

The green snake is long. The red snake is short.

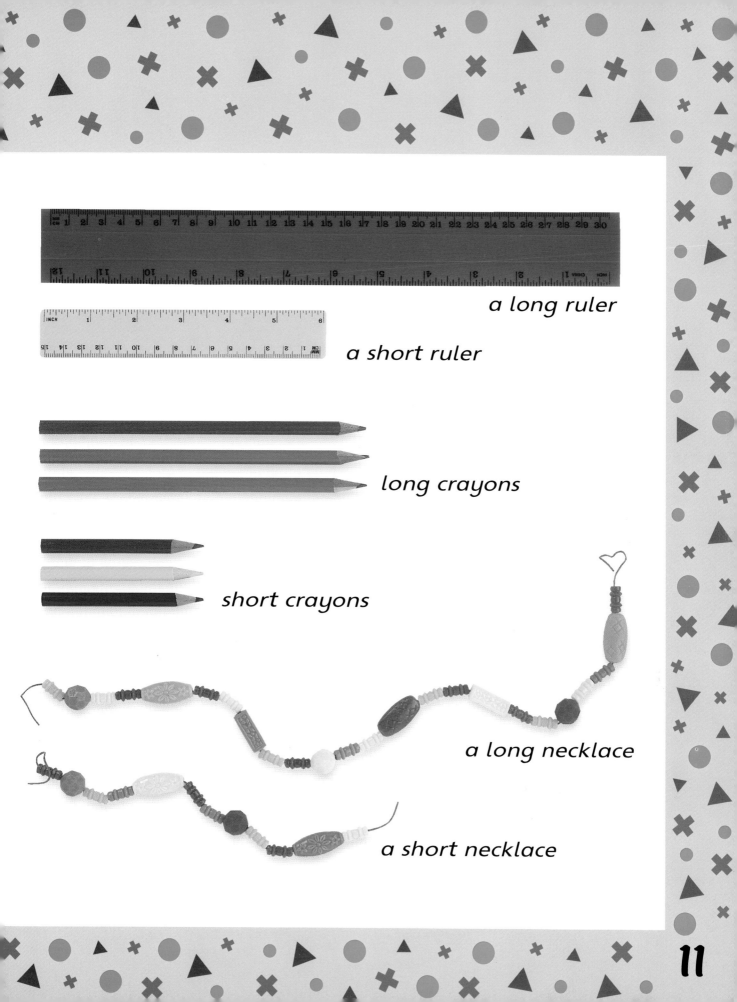

a long ruler

a short ruler

long crayons

short crayons

a long necklace

a short necklace

longer and shorter

This train is longer than me.

See if you can find something that is longer than you.

This train is shorter than me.

Can you find something that is shorter than you?

wide and narrow

Wide and narrow are to do with the size of things from one side to the other.

The red book is wide. The blue book is narrow.

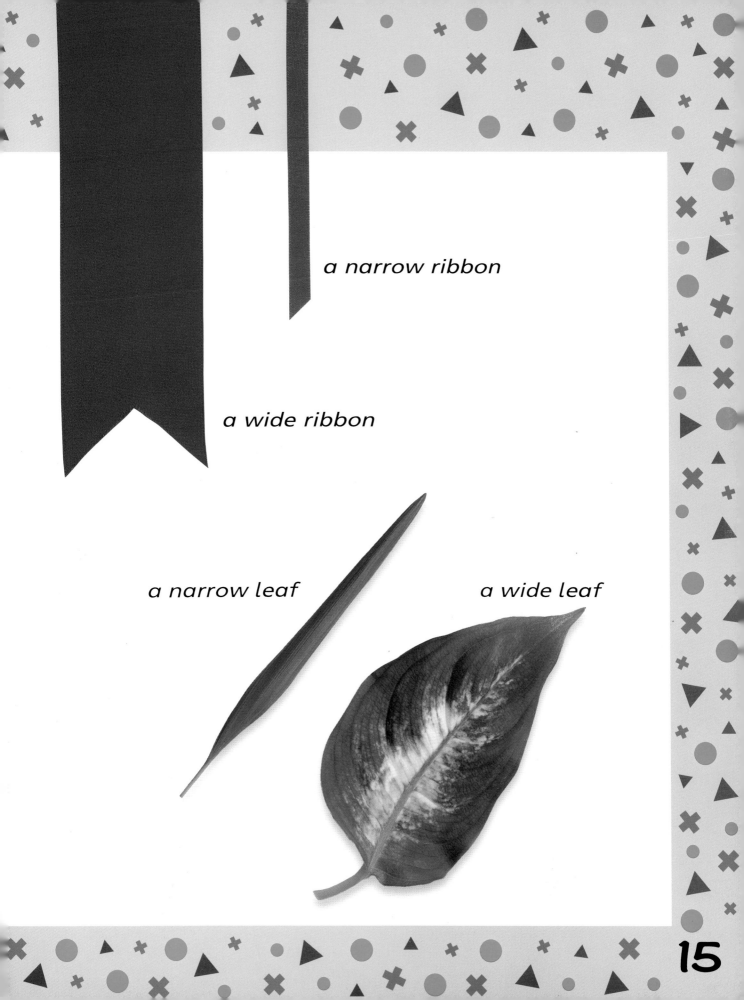

a narrow ribbon

a wide ribbon

a narrow leaf

a wide leaf

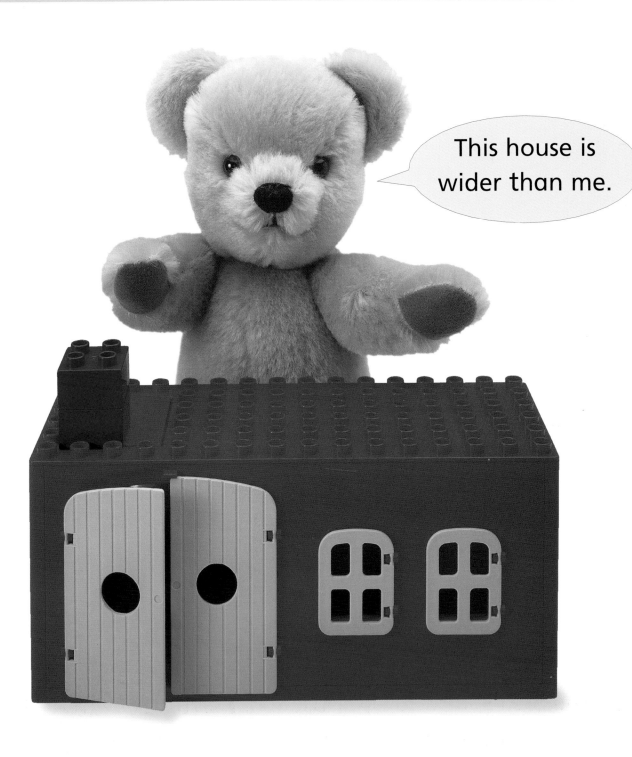

The doors in a doll's house are narrower than you.
The doors in your own house are wider than you!

big and small

Big things take up more space than small things.

The red car is big. The yellow car is small.

a big tipper truck

a small tipper truck

a big purse

a small purse

bigger and smaller

This ball is bigger than me!

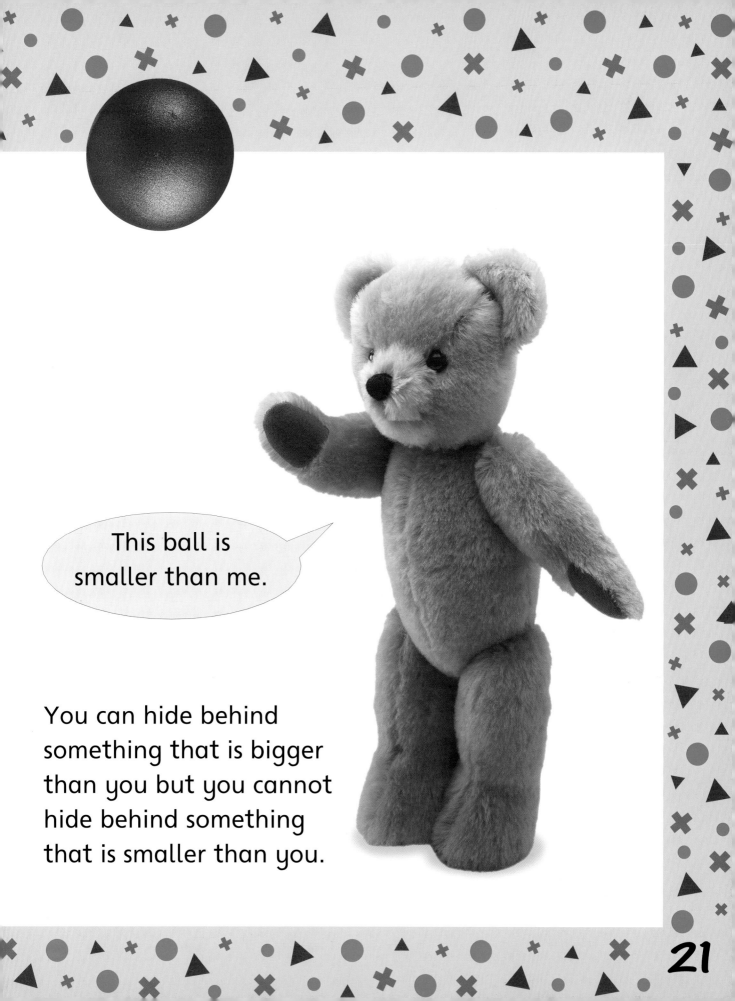

This ball is smaller than me.

You can hide behind something that is bigger than you but you cannot hide behind something that is smaller than you.

What size is it?

You can compare these toys to Marmaduke. Use size words to describe them.

For example, the boat is narrower and shorter than Marmaduke.

Why not use size words
to compare these toys
to each other?

glossary

compare look at things to see how they are different

describe say what something looks like

example an idea or object that shows the sort of thing you mean

ruler an object used to measure how long things are

tipper truck a truck, or lorry, with a back part that lifts up and tips out its load

index